Leadershi

Clergy and Lay Leadership in the Local Church

Chris Skilton

Team Rector of Sanderstead

GROVE BOOKS LIMITED
RIDLEY HALL RD CAMBRIDGE CB3 9HU

Contents

Acknowledgements
I should like to thank the members of the Grove Pastoral Group for their encouragement and advice in the production of this booklet and particularly the Rev Nick Helm for his helpful comments.

The Cover Illustration is by Peter Ashton

First Impression June 1999
ISSN 0144-171X
ISBN 1 85174 404 5

1
Introduction

A Personal Conviction

In the nineteen years that I have been ordained I have been a curate, team vicar and team rector in four different churches. Each one has had a leadership team of some form, and each has been differently constituted and differently named. I have been part of an eldership, a ministry team, CREW (clergy, reader and wardens) and a wider team. I cannot imagine being in full-time ordained ministry without being part of a team.

In recent years I have talked with leaders and members of teams from a variety of contexts. Most were begun as informal arrangements initiated by the incumbent and church council. Increasingly, dioceses with schemes for Ordained Local Ministry (OLM) have made the presence of a ministry team a prerequisite for the parish receiving the OLM onto the staff of the church.[1]

But there is no national or diocesan forum, as far as I know, for team members to receive training or advice. The diocesan schemes do have a Ministry Development Officer (or equivalent) who helps set up the teams and does troubleshooting when required. But informal teams begun in the last thirty years or so have no such place to turn.

This booklet seeks to raise the issues related to leadership teams—the clergy and lay teams set up to share in the work of leadership and pastoral oversight in the local church. The term most often refers to English Anglican practice but there are parallels in other denominations.

The first part of the booklet seeks to put leadership teams in a contemporary, biblical and theological context, giving pointers for areas of discussion in the local church. This will help teams to be seen in the light of Christian conviction and tradition—not just as a passing fad or a pragmatic response to a current problem.

These chapters should be read before moving to the more practical issues in the second part.

1 Southwark diocese, for instance, makes this an essential part of a parish sponsoring and receiving an OLM.

2
Why Leadership Teams?

Without a question, we have moved some way from the church structures wholly dominated by clergy that prevailed up until the end of the Second World War. Following are some of the factors that have combined to create a climate welcoming to shared leadership teams.

Cultural Expectations

A shift in the way in which we view hierarchical structures has been well-charted across political, social and national life. This has touched the church profoundly in theology, organization and liturgy[2]: witness 1960s' radicalism, the formation of the General Synod and the liturgical change leading to the *Alternative Service Book* and beyond. Without this climate of change, it is doubtful whether teams would have ever emerged.

New Ways of Doing Church

The 1950s' missions by Billy Graham produced ordinands who entered the church from outside and were thus unaware of past structures and ways of working. Since then, patterns of training and styles of ministry within the church have become increasingly diverse. The 'Clergy House' presided over by 'the Incumbent with his (*sic*) curates' has given way to a world of colleagues and training agreements. Authorized ministries and lay training courses have proliferated, opening up new opportunities for lay involvement in the life of the church. Pastoral assistants, youth workers and parish administrators are examples of lay people in high-profile leadership roles in the local church.

Pragmatism

Some pressure for change and collaboration has been openly finance-driven in the 1990s. Dioceses have advocated change in parish life to meet a decrease in full-time stipendiary clergy and a lack of resources to pay them. This has been especially true in rural and UPA areas. Whatever the financial position, these initiatives should be affirmed as good for the church.

Contemporary Thinking about Changing Leadership

At least four factors have fuelled the drive towards shared ministry and leadership in the last 35 years. These strands suggest that lay leadership has emerged as a significant change of emphasis in the ordering of the church.

2 Grace Davie, *Religion in Britain Since 1945* (Oxford: Blackwell, 1994) is a helpful summary of the issues.

1. Roman Catholic Thinking

Yves Congar, Hans Kung, Vincent Donovan and Eduard Schillebecckx have all written about the important place of each individual baptized believer within the life of the local church.[3] Although marginalized by the hierarchy of their church, their writings have been taken up by Catholics and non-Catholics alike as serious theological engagement with the meaning of the church and especially the role of laity.

2. The Rise of Evangelicals in the Church of England

The number of evangelical churches has grown significantly in the past 30 years.[4] This wing of the church is most open to expressing the idea of the ministry of every member of the local church—at least in theory! Although it may not always work out in practice, more and more churches are likely to travel down this road.

3. The Charismatic Movement

Insights from the charismatic movement now play a part in the mainstream life of the Church of England. Two favourite texts of the movement, 1 Corinthians 12 and Ephesians 4, are being read with a new urgency and application for the church. More people are seen to be empowered with gifts for ministry. Gifting of each individual by the grace of God is seen as equally valid to the ordination of some (and in some quarters more so).

4. Base Communities

Originally grass-roots Roman Catholic communities in South America, these base communities depend on lay leaders. Their primary emphasis is on shared study and prayer arising out of and leading into action. Tasks and ministries are apportioned to all members of the community.

Although it is difficult to compare these communities with anything similar in Britain, they are a significant example of a wider movement towards the empowering of small groups not dependent on clergy. Small groups have given people the opportunity to lead activities once reserved for the clergy alone.

3 See Yves Congar, *Lay People in the Church* (London: Geoffrey Chapman, 1965); Hans Kung, *Why Priests* (London, 1972); Vincent Donovan, *Christianity Rediscovered* (London: SCM, 1978); Eduard Schillebecckx, *The Church with a Human Face* (London: SCM, 1985).

4 Michael Saward in *Evangelicals on the Move* (Oxford: Mowbray, 1987) charts this development.

3
The Biblical Material

Old Testament Perspectives

There is no single biblical blueprint for leadership in one particular form. But through the different periods of the life of the people of God, there is a common understanding of Yahweh as the one who leads his people. Jacob's blessing of Joseph (Genesis 48.15), the praise of the psalmist (Psalm 78.52) and the prophecy of Hosea (Hosea 11.1–4) all speak of a God who leads. This theological conviction, however, has varied expression in human government, as we see below.

- Dominant personalities such as Moses have ruled by the authority of God.
- In the period of the Judges, individuals were charismatically endowed to lead loose confederations of tribes (Judges 3.9; 6.11–12).
- Leadership in the settled state of Israel was vested in the king, yet prophets, priests and wise men had their own areas of controlling influence (Isaiah 1.23ff; Jeremiah 23.14ff).
- A strong royalist theology is expressed in some psalms (Psalms 2 and 72 for instance).
- The independent prophets pronounced God's judgment on those in authority who failed to deliver appropriate leadership. The authority of the leaders failed when they did not lead people according to God's standards (1 Kings 21.20ff; Micah 3).
- Elders were set aside to assist Moses, especially in the administration of justice (Numbers 11.16ff) during the wilderness wanderings. They retained a role in settled society (1 Kings 12.8; Isaiah 3.2) but this is never defined.

Over several centuries no clear mandate emerges for one definitive expression in human institutions of Israel's convictions about the leadership of God. A summary of good models of Old Testament leadership sees them as those having, 'the ability to attract others to a worthwhile cause, align these followers in the same direction, encourage them to express their particular talents, and sustain a common vision in the face of considerable obstacles.'[5]

New Testament Models

Ministry in the New Testament looks back to the life of Jesus. His ministry is a life of humble activity, carrying no special rights or powers (Matthew 23.11; Luke 22.27). Servanthood is the key quality, as reflected in Mark 10.45, a vital text for understanding Jesus' ministry: 'Even the Son of Man did not come to be served, but to serve and to give his life as a ransom for many.' The relationship between the Father and the Son is now to be lived out between the Son and his disciples

5 Richard Higginson, *Transforming Leadership* (London: SPCK, 1996) p 31.

(John 20.19–24). The twelve were trained in service, not as managers or church leaders, but to live with the risen Christ as their head.

A fluid and diverse picture of ministry emerges from a study of the early church's life. What happened in, say, Jerusalem, Antioch and Ephesus[6] was shaped around common principles but without any early co-ordination—no New Testament writer or church leader sat down to plan a universal order for church government. There was no single way of organizing church and no attempt to harmonize the patterns of ministry between churches.

We find that a local ministry was exercised by the whole body, alongside the external ministry of an apostle by letter-writing or visit.[7] However, by the end of the first century there was a growing institutionalizing of forms of ministry. Within a short time Ignatius could write of a college of presbyters and Polycarp of the orders of presbyters and deacons in Philippi.[8] Schillebecckx calls this a shift from the charisma of the many to the charisma of the few—a specialization by individuals of what belonged communally to everyone.[9]

In setting up a leadership team there are important principles to grasp from Scripture. These include:

- oversight and servanthood exercised following the example of Jesus;
- ministry shared by the whole body;
- a diversity of local leaders by virtue of function and gift, relating to an overriding external authority;
- leaders who are part of the body, called above all to relationship with Christ and his people rather than to particular tasks;
- unity of the people valued above the practice of gifts;
- no class of people deemed to possess certain rights or powers; and
- leadership in plurality.

Eldership?

It is worth looking at the biblical basis for the term 'eldership,' as some churches today use it to describe their leadership teams. 'Elders' as a group have a place in Judaism from a very early date through to the first century (Exodus 3.18; Joshua 7.6; 1 Kings 8.1; Jeremiah 26.17; Ezra 8.11) in supporting the leader of the nation. They also exist in the government of the synagogue in Jesus' day (Luke 7.3).

The early church in Jerusalem is described initially as having 'apostles' for its leadership, but Luke later refers to 'apostles and elders' (Acts 15.2). He assumes that his readers know what he means by this! The term could have been borrowed from the local synagogue or simply could have been a term of esteem for the church's founders. In the churches addressed in 1 Peter there is a settled ministry

6 Prophets and teachers in Antioch (Acts 13.1); apostles and elders at Jerusalem (Acts 15.2); elders at Ephesus (Acts 20.17).
7 Contrast Romans 12.6–8 and 2 Corinthians 1.23–2.4.
8 Ignatius, *To the Smyrneans* 8; Polycarp, *Ad Phil* 5.3.
9 Schillebecckx, *op cit*, p 121.

of elders who exercise oversight (1 Peter 5.1, 2), but Paul makes very little use of the word.[10]

There are certainly biblical examples of elders (always used in the plural), but this is simply one of a variety of ways of describing corporate leadership. A church that uses the term today can claim biblical precedence for its use, but needs to spell out precisely what is meant. It is not accurate to describe it as 'the biblical model' or 'a return to the New Testament pattern' for leadership.[11]

10 There are references to 'elders' in the Pastoral Epistles but the dispute as to their authorship is well known. In Ephesus, there is a well-established group of elders (1 Tim 5.17–19), some (but not all of them) having a teaching function.

11 There is a helpful discussion of this issue in Michael Saward's *All Change* (London: Hodder & Stoughton, 1983) pp 44–46.

4
Theological Considerations

Very few of the churches I contacted had foundation documents or written material to share with the congregation about the origin of their team. Even diocesan OLM schemes are not terribly good at 'showing their working out,' although they do better on the group processes that come next. This is especially true of theological reflection on leadership teams. Using a current phrase, it 'isn't sexy enough' to attract or warrant attention.

However, I would strongly urge those considering or starting a team to engage with at least the biblical and theological issues I raise and to read some of the material I refer to. Existing teams, too, would benefit from revisiting—or even getting acquainted with—these foundations.

Baptism and the People of God

Baptism, Eucharist and Ministry (the LIMA text) describes baptism as 'the sign and seal of our common discipleship.'[12] From this premise, it suggests that ministry is shared by the whole baptized people of God. Ordained ministers fulfil their calling only in and for the Christian community.

Through their baptism, ordained ministers share in the ministry of the whole people. They may exercise this in particular ways, but there should be a legitimate sharing in leadership between clergy and laity. Leadership can be shared because no-one can be said to inherit, purchase or claim an inalienable right to it.[13]

This view requires a 'strong' view of baptism, understanding it to be full Christian initiation. To see it as anything less may lead to ordination being understood as a supplement to what was given at baptism only to the privileged few 'professionals.' A lack of clear baptismal instruction that does not spell out the ministry responsibilities or the gifts to enable ministry is a dangerous policy.

Talk of baptism may seem a long way from leadership! However, the commissioning of every baptized believer to share in the ministry of the local church includes the potential for its members to receive gifts appropriate for leadership.

The Nature of Ministry

Convictions about the nature of ministry help to undergird thinking about leadership teams. These must begin from a belief that ministry at its heart is theological and not utilitarian or pragmatic. The recent Board of Mission Occasional Paper, *A Time for Sharing,* stated that ministry is rooted in the nature of God as

12 WCC, *Baptism, Eucharist and Ministry* (Geneva: WCC, 1982). See Baptism D 6, p 3.
13 The whole section on 'Ministry' repays study, but see especially I 5 (p 20); II A 12 (p 22) and II C 17 (p 23).

Trinity: 'The character of God is a model of that perfection to which the Spirit draws us; hence dominance, subservience or isolation are not only immoral, but a theological wrong against the God who creates, redeems and sustains us.'[14]

There is a shape to Christian ministry that precedes any particular form of it. Tom Torrance writes of how the church's life and order remain contingent on the finished work of Christ. He says, 'The church looks upon its ordering in the space and time of this ongoing world as the required form of its obedience to Christ or the attestation of its reliance upon the new Covenant founded for ever in the historical Jesus.'[15]

Churches wishing to take reflection about shared leadership seriously will find the following texts helpful for insight into working out what ministry in the local church means today. Each is written from a very different perspective and tradition. In a balanced team, different ones would appeal to different members.

1. Ian Bunting: *Models for Ministry*[16]

This Grove booklet begins where many churches are—with the clergy and their role. Bunting is critical of clergy-dominated models or those that promote the specialist skills of one person alone. He is aware that models that actively embrace laity may scare many clergy away.

His preferred option for Christian leadership is the 'pathfinder' model. The pathfinder leads the way in and for the Christian community. This model preserves the place of distinctive leadership but shows that it only makes sense in relation to the Christian community. It requires collaboration, sees shared leadership as essential and offers a structure in which it would work well.

2. Robin Greenwood: *Transforming Priesthood*[17]

Greenwood's vision of ministry is rooted in the belief that God calls all humankind and creation into relationship to share in his ultimate purpose, which is community. The ordained priest is a member of the eucharistic community whose function is to preside in it. The priest therefore retains a pivotal role in leading and sustaining the network of relationships in that community.

Ministry is shared by all the members and is rooted in the very being of the church. He writes, 'as a celebration of Christ's own uniting presence, the church requires an ordained ministry that models inter-dependence and mutuality with the laity and between all the ordained.'[18]

Greenwood's practical outworking is rather clerically focused. However, his work is an important attempt to explore how shared leadership is to be grounded

14 Board of Mission, *A Time for Sharing* (Occasional Paper 6, London: Board of Mission, 1995).
15 Tom Torrance, 'The Ministry' in Ray Anderson (ed), *Theological Foundations for Ministry* (Edinburgh: T & T Clark, 1979).
16 Ian Bunting, *Models for Ministry* (Grove Pastoral Series No 54, Cambridge: Grove Books, 1993) pp 21–23.
17 Robin Greenwood, *Transforming Priesthood* (London: SPCK, 1994).
18 *ibid*, p 164

in theological reflection. It is also important as a study from a more catholic tradition. This voice needs to be heard if shared leadership is to be expressed across a wide churchmanship.

3. John Tiller: *A Strategy for the Church's Ministry* [19]

Tiller's report is the earliest of the three studies to be published, but current concerns about a lack of full-time stipendiary clergy have brought the ideas to prominence again. He calls for a radical change in the pattern of the church's ministry so that lay people can share more fully in ministry and leadership roles. Typical is his assertion that

> the liturgy requires a president, the decision-making process requires a chairman and congregational oversight requires a pastor.... [T]here are no compelling reasons why the roles of president, chairman and pastor have to be ordained—or why any of them may not be shared.[20]

Ministry is described as being firstly local, with leadership shared in the life of the church. There is, however, no suggestion of how the local leader(s) should emerge or how oversight should be shared amongst local congregation, priest and bishop.

These three approaches indicate a growing desire to explore how theological convictions ought to shape the leadership of the local church. Those exploring initiating a shared leadership team should study at least one attempt to set out a theological rationale. They need not necessarily embrace it, but should at least see how the work is done. Any scheme should have the foundations in place as well as the structure. Preferably this should be dug out by the church itself—or at least thoughtfully borrowed from another builder.

19 John Tiller, *A Strategy for the Church's Ministry* (London: CIO Publishing, 1983).
20 *ibid*, para 110, p 63.

5
Getting Started

Before tackling the practical issues, it is worth asking if you have thought through the biblical and theological issues at staff and PCC level—and read the first part of the booklet.

The Starting Point

Each church already has a shared leadership team in its church council of clergy and laity. The churchwardens also have certain legal functions that they discharge working alongside the Incumbent. We will return to this later.

Is It Worth It?

Like so many issues in church life, this question needs to be asked—and answered honestly. Being a member of a team can be a time-consuming business. It may tie up people who would be better using their gifts in other ways. And it may not be appropriate at a particular stage of a church's life. For instance, a small struggling church surfacing from a crisis may need careful, directive leadership from one or two people for a short spell.

There must be clear, expected and known benefits to the church in setting up and running a team, for there is no guarantee of success. Teams can produce very different responses. One incumbent said, 'if such schemes are carefully prepared, the benefits are out of all proportion to the problems incurred.'[21] But another said, 'I sensed that many thought a monster had been created with the team.'[22] There must be a prior conviction that a church will run better and will more faithfully model being 'church' if it has a leadership team.

What Is the Team For?

Deciding a team's purpose is a vital part of the preparatory process and will help shape the composition of the team. Some teams that I spoke to had very clear reasons for the shape of their team. One came into existence as an extension of the leadership and pastoral responsibility entrusted to the vicar. Another stated, 'Elders were appointed in the New Testament churches and were a corporate body, no one elder was ever expected to carry the responsibility for oversight alone.'[23] All

21 Saward, *Evangelicals on the Move*, p 58

22 From private correspondence with an incumbent after his arrival in the parish. Where the information has been gathered in this way, confidentiality has been retained. Some accounts of teams have been written up and published, and are worth study, including Michael Saward, *All Change* (see above); John P Baker, *Christ's Living Body* (London: Coverdale, 1973); Cyril Ashton, *Church on the Threshold* (London: Daybreak/DLT, 1991 edition); Robin Greenwood, *Reclaiming the Church* (London: Collins, Fount Paperbacks, 1988).

23 From private correspondence.

the teams expressed the importance of sharing and extending leadership to a wider body than the incumbent (and other clergy).

There are other spoken and unspoken reasons, such as support for the clergy, coping with ministry needs, because it is right and because the diocese requires it. Whilst there is no 'correct' answer for existence, there should be an expressed purpose, agreed by the PCC and the team.

Methods of Appointment

Churches have found a variety of ways of appointing members, sometimes combining two or more of these as part of the process:

By the Incumbent and Staff Team—with or without the Churchwardens

This may include seeking the approval of the PCC but can still give the impression of being 'the vicar's group.' However, as part of the strategic development of a church an incumbent may need to be able to pick a team to lead it forward in a particular way. An incumbent may ask for the opportunity to choose a balanced team of people who can work together.

By Consultation with the Church

In one church, members of the congregation were asked to submit names to the incumbent, who then made recommendations to the PCC on this basis. The whole church is involved in the process—but only one person knows to what extent.

By Election

This is the most democratic means but also the most hazardous. It would be especially dangerous in churches where there are damaging tensions and serious unresolved conflicts. Election allows no opportunity to think strategically about the shape and composition of the team.

By Virtue of Office or Appointment

This makes clear as to who belongs to the team—usually the clergy, readers, pastoral assistants and lay workers. As these individuals have an authorized public ministry in the church, they will already have been commended for their work by the church council and may be licensed or authorized by a bishop. If churchwardens are included, they will have been elected at the annual meeting.

Whilst there has been a clear mandate for this group to work in their approved areas of ministry, this is not necessarily qualification for membership of the team. A church following this pattern may need to take this into consideration when electing wardens or commending people for authorized ministry.

The Heads of Department

The co-ordinators of pastoral care, evangelism and youth work, along with housegroup leaders, are the sort of people who might form a team with the clergy (and wardens). There is a clear logic to this group meeting to co-ordinate issues relating to the life and development of the church. However, this sort of grouping may find themselves encroaching on the work of the PCC.

Other qualifications

Some churches mentioned seeking the qualities recommended in 1 Timothy 5 and Titus 2. These chapters certainly set a high standard for Christian leadership but it is not clear whether they can be directly applied to these groups of people.

One church mentioned 'length of membership of the church' and 'likely commitment to the area' as qualifications. These terms are not quantified and would be fine in a very settled area, but a church with a transient population could struggle with this.

One church mentioned a retiring age of 70 (and with a five-year term) implying that no one over 65 would be appointed! Other churches said 'for life.'

A few years ago some churches were specifying men only for leadership teams. This is gradually changing as we have moved into an era where gender neither qualifies or disqualifies for ministry in the church. The place of women in leadership positions still needs to be addressed by a church—especially as acceptance of its logic does not always square with the emotional response.

Leaving the Team

This is not a priority when just starting a team but is an issue that needs to be clear from the beginning. Leaving can be a far more hazardous process than joining. Some members will leave when their term of office as churchwarden comes to an end or when they retire as reader or step down as housegroup co-ordinator. One or two teams have fixed terms of office that may be renewable by the Incumbent, the PCC or the team itself. Some simply say that members are on the team 'until the person thinks it right or personal circumstances dictate it.'

A team could become a strong clique if there were no change in its membership for ten years or more. There will need to be a clearly prescribed way for people to cease being a member of the team and adequate preparation for the team, the church and the leaving member.

The Significance of the Name

The name of the team sends clear signals to the congregation about the nature of the group. Some that I have found in use are:

- **Pastoral team** This is fine if it is actually what the group does. But in one case it may not have squared with their declared task of 'seeking the Lord's vision for the local church.'
- **Elders** The discussion in chapter 2 details the history of the term and the care with which it needs to be exercised today. There may be good reasons for a church to choose the word, but this should be done only after careful teaching to show how it does and does not resonate with the biblical term.

- **Ministry team** This is commonly in use and describes what the team does. It can imply that 'real' ministry is done by the group and can be as excluding as the clergy / laity divide. An important question is whether the group releases the whole church for ministry or sucks everything into it.
- **Staff team** This may be descriptive if it is accurate. It may blur distinctions between clergy and laity, paid and voluntary.
- **Clergy, reader and wardens (known as 'CREW')** This is clumsy, ugly, memorable and accurate.
- **Leadership team** There is a directness about the title and a focus on its purpose. The PCC might also want to claim that role for itself.
- **Leadership and oversight group** This term has the same directness as the term, 'leadership team.' I am not sure that I would want 'LOG' as an acronym because of its associations with 'log jams' or thickness.
- **Wider team** This is the name of the group I inherited and belong to at the moment. It is intended to be expressive of its membership of clergy, readers, pastoral assistants and wardens. But some people may have forgotten what it is 'wider' than!

No single name seems ideal; all have their problems. Nevertheless it is important to teach the congregation and those beyond which name is used and why—and to revisit those reasons and statements regularly.

Size

Most teams find that 10-12 members is an optimum and maximum number—after all there is a precedent! A larger group tends to lose a sense of cohesiveness, identity and ability to relate. This may pose a problem in a large church with numerous readers or lay assistants. Alternatively, a group of four or five may show great commitment to one another and to the task, but the hard work for such a small number may put a great strain on the members.

Aims and Goals

Nothing is likely to cause more suspicion and distrust than a group of the church leaders who meets regularly but has no declared aims or goals. Of the churches I contacted very few had written statements of a team's aims. An agreed statement works wonders for helping the congregation begin to see what a group is for. It is also vital for the group to share common aims and goals.

One team's stated aim is to 'work together to oversee the life of the church and to ensure that the church works on a "mission" model, not a pastoral one.'[24] That is fine—as long as the current members of the group own that aim and the congregation has it before them. All of this needs to be agreed before a team is established. Time spent doing this will save much time later if difficult tangles emerge.

24 From private correspondence.

6
Maintaining Team Life

There should be no illusion that a team can be left to run itself once established. Maintaining team life is the responsibility of all its members. On a basic level the members must have an understanding as to when the team meets, how often and for how long. The meetings should not be so frequent (for example, weekly) that it saps the life out of the group and cuts them off from other church members, their families or their wider interests. Nor should it be so infrequent that the team has no opportunity to learn to work together.

Clearly some evenings are better for some people than for others. But the regular choice of, say, the third Tuesday of the month may always put particular pressure on one member. This sounds obvious but needs to be said and agreed.

Practical Issues

A range of other small details can make a difference to the life of the team. Where the team meets says something about its nature. If it always gathers at the vicarage that tells the members about where is safe territory for the incumbent! There needs to be agreement about who chairs the meeting—is it automatically the Incumbent? Who chairs it when he or she is ill or away—the curate? the churchwarden? an appointed deputy?

Paperwork can cause problems. Most members of a group like some advanced notice of what they are going to be talking about. This could be in the form of an agenda or simply a list of issues that need discussion in the next few meetings. Who creates this or has access to it says something about the group.

The same applies to minutes or notes of the meeting. Someone needs to be appointed to write these—if there are to be any. It needs to be clear whether these are formal minutes that need 'agreeing' at the next meeting and who has access to them. They could be public documents or private memory-joggers for the group.

Confidentiality and collective responsibility are vital principles for agreement. The group must have freedom to discuss a range of viewpoints and ideas, but there must be clear 'rules' about accountability for those outside of the group. Failure to follow agreed procedures could be disastrous for the life and well-being of the church.

Getting each of these issues right means establishing the right way of working, agreed and practised by the whole team. To do so will save a lot of time—and future heartaches.

Team Life and Processes

Putting a team together is not just about having the best individuals but about how the team works together. Effective groups develop when each member contributes to the common tasks and to the life of the group. Meredith

Belbin has written from a secular viewpoint about how teams succeed or fail.[25] He suggests that badly composed teams 'tend to fail in the end.'[26]

Belbin even goes so far as to conclude that teamsmanship transcends fitness for any particular role and is as important as any specialized ability that a team member might possess. Clearly there are problems when a team is appointed by virtue of office, because then there is less control over their team suitability. However, even to acknowledge one's skills and the possible gaps in a team is a big step forward.

For instance, I have worked in a team that had a number of members who were gifted in initiating projects and thinking about possibilities for the future. There was, however, no-one whose first gifts were for seeing projects through to their close (a 'Completer-Finisher' in Belbin's terms[27]). In recognizing this we could take stock of how we were going to ensure that initiatives were seen through to completion, given that none of us was especially skilled at that. And other facilities such as the Myers-Briggs Personality Type Indicator can help teams discover their make up and determine where the team may have to compensate for under-representation.

Teams will benefit by learning from secular management structures, techniques and insights. Charles Handy has done much to popularize these and make them accessible to a wide range of people. Team members could profitably read one of his books and discuss how their team might implement some of his findings.[28]

There will undoubtedly be a tension between wanting to see the church as a dynamic, living body and treating it as 'another organization.' Yet it is helpful to acknowledge that it shares many features with secular organizations and thus can gain insights from them.

As with so many areas of team life, there is no magic formula. Handy and others recognize that a structure is essential to make possible the effective performance of key activities.[29] Yet there is no ideal best structure out there waiting to be encompassed. In any given situation there will be the best structure for a specific team to undertake the task at hand.

Organizing Team Life

Given that the dynamics of team life are important to its working smoothly and effectively, how much members of the team understand and value the group processes will be significant for the way the team operates.

For instance, it is reckoned that although a group produces fewer ideas than the sum of the individuals present, those ideas are usually better because they are

25 Meredith Belbin, *Management Teams: Why they Succeed or Fail* (Oxford: Butterworth/Heinemann, 1981).

26 *ibid*, p 85.

27 Belbin lists eight useful types of people to have in a team on p 78.

28 Charles Handy, *Understanding Organizations* (London: Penguin, 1993, 4th edition) and Charles Handy, *Understanding Voluntary Organizations* (London: Penguin, 1988).

29 Handy, *Understanding Organizations*, pp 97ff.

evaluated and thought through in the group. If the team members know and understand this, they will be better able to develop ideas while being less frustrated about not coming up with more possibilities.

Both experience and management study suggest that team work brings a sense of belonging, mutual understanding and support. Properly managed, the group experience offers great benefits to the members, the performance of the task and the outcome of the process.

Working together can mean a lot to the members. In the church context, this will probably mean opportunities for Bible study, discussion and prayer. The value of meals together and the occasional 48-hour residential time cannot be underestimated. For often it is at team meetings that church leaders can say the unsayable and think the unthinkable without compromising their public role.

Needless to say, confidentiality is crucial. Members of the team often treasure the support that they have received in their private life, their work life and their church life through being part of the group. In one team I have worked in (made up of people by virtue of their office), those who left the team at the end of their term said that leaving the team produced a far greater sense of loss than stepping down as churchwarden or pastoral assistant.

All does not always go so well. Alarmingly, no leadership team that I have spoken to had a consultant who could assist with the process of the team, but one clearly wished that it had. Whilst there is so much that can be good in a team, problems can be disastrous for the life of the whole church. One team admitted:, 'We did run into real problems which were due to the internal group process.'[30]

This is a salutary warning about the importance of thinking carefully about how the team 'works,' as well as what issues it should discuss and what roles to perform. It means attending with care to the practical issues outlined here and ensuring that procedures are defined and agreed.

From time to time the team should take stock of how meetings are run—both officially and unofficially. This includes looking at who speaks and who is quiet; how disagreements are handled and resolved (or not resolved); and where the authority lies. A team must work at the process constantly, not in order to spend many an evening navel-gazing, but to ensure that the process leads the team to serve the church and the kingdom more effectively.

30 From private correspondence.

7
Issues to Work On

In the life of a team several issues seem to recur that can reduce the effectiveness of its working. They also significantly increase the time and energy that are needed to manage the team. Given current Anglican structures, these issues will not go away, but if we are aware of them, strategies can be devised for handling them.

Leadership

This issue lies under the surface of several areas of concern. I have already posed the question of whether shared leadership can give concrete expression to a notion of authority modelled on Christ. Chapter 4 suggests a way forward.

Shared leadership could be used to avoid facing up to responsibility and accountability. A team needs a focus, both within the church and more importantly, beyond it. There can be tension between the reality of shared leadership and the public face of the church.

John Moore, writing in *A Time for Sharing*, observes that 'At an anecdotal level, the most effective churches I have seen have been where there is strong collaborative ministry.'[31] But he notes that this is also focused in one person who has 'ensured people know what the team's task is and has enabled them to achieve it. [Such individuals] act as what someone once described as "agents of coherence and purpose."'[32]

Whilst it is customary for the incumbent to be 'the leader' and the 'executor of decisions,' this is not *essential* for the office. If it were to be the case, it would take a great deal of preparatory work in the church and beyond.

Shared leadership is not a retreat from strong leadership. Advocacy of every-member ministry and shared leadership should not be taken as an attempt to downgrade leaders in the church's life. Nor should either be seen as an attempt to replace proper spiritual authority with democratic consensus.

Leadership must be seen as a function of the Christian community, not as status over and against it. The community needs leadership because of the theological demands of the Christian faith as well as the organizational demands of a human institution.

Gifts of grace mark out a Christian leader, which we have noted before: the call to follow the example and pattern of Jesus; an acceptance of the Holy Spirit's empowerment for service; and a calling from God the Father to serve in the name of God the Trinity. Quite often in the church we see Christian character being formed before leadership is assumed.

31 John Moore writing in *A Time for Sharing*, p 27.
32 *ibid.*

That is not to say naively that because the team are all decent Christians, everything will be all right. But it is to accept that a balance between Christian belief and practice and an understanding of how organizations and institutions work will affect how leadership functions.

The Relationship between Clergy and Lay Members of the Team

The leadership team may engender fear in traditionally trained clergy—and others. There may be fear of competition, of losing recognition and status or of weaknesses being exposed. In some areas there could be a transfer of work and, most significantly, of authority. Currently this is mainly asked of clergy who have voluntarily set up teams. But this will change with the requirement of some dioceses for a team to be in place where an OLM ministers.

It may be necessary to redefine an Incumbent's role in the light of team ministry. Could it end up like a chaplain or liturgical functionary? Robin Greenwood believes that Incumbents always have an ongoing responsibility to teach, co-ordinate and preside. He suggests it would be possible for them to exercise 'an authority which is primarily a spiritual one,' although he concedes 'that it is inevitable that a parish priest will sometimes feel convinced of the need to exert pressure, subtle or otherwise, to lead the parish in a particular direction.'[33]

Different contexts bring different issues. In a large suburban parish, the Incumbent may very easily be able to assume this teaching, co-ordinating, presiding role. However, what of a country village where the clergy are present one part of a day of a week and every other Sunday? Could it be that the churchwardens are effectively the presidents of that community, and the clergy are only an occasional, liturgical functionary? How might a team work in that situation?

The introduction of a leadership team affects other structures in the parish as well. A team is not a bolt-on optional extra but a radical change in how the church lives and works.

For instance, a number of churches have teams whereby each member is assigned responsibility for a geographical area of the parish. This brings up such issues as whether that responsibility is to the congregation who are resident or to the local population. There needs to be a clear understanding as to whether this affects the role the Incumbent plays in that area.

Questions that might be asked include, Is the team member visiting 'on behalf of the church'?; should the incumbent inform the team member before making any visits in that area? These are not insuperable problems but provide a good example of issues that need clarifying.

Two interesting secular models can help in defining the role of clergy in a team. David Steele cites the example of US mayors. Their responsibilities are largely ceremonial but also require representing the city to itself and to outside entities.

33 Robin Greenwood, 'Presiding: a Parish Priest's Work,' *Theology* 87 (1984) p 417.

This requires personal charism, carries accountability and involves shared authority as the presiding officer of the council.[34]

Or John Harvey-Jones's description of a chairman of the board may be of help. He sets out five key features of the role: to ensure that the company adds up to more than the sum of its parts; to set long-term vision and aspiration; to set the organization's values and tempo; to represent the public face of the company; and to exemplify the values the company claims to embrace.[35]

There will also be a need, where appropriate, to consider the role and position of a curate, NSMs or OLMs in the team. There needs to be a clear understanding as to whether these individuals are automatically members of the team. This may affect the commonly held diocesan view about the particular relationship between the training incumbent and curate. The team may also want a say in the appointment of junior and non-stipendiary clergy.

Relationship with Other Statutory Bodies

The relationship between teams and other bodies is an area where problems can arise. A key question is the relationship between the team and the PCC. From the beginning clear boundaries need to be established, reviewed regularly and not crossed intentionally. The PCC is the decision-making body and the team has an advisory role.

The team might, for instance, discuss the pastoral implications of changing the time of the main morning service and consider who might be adversely affected by it and how the church and its leaders should handle the situation. It may even have a recommendation to make. But any decision must be made by the PCC, and this must be a 'real' decision made after proper discussion. The PCC is not there to rubber stamp a decision already made by the team.

Having all the team members on the PCC has advantages and disadvantages. It gives a sense of accountability to have them there, but other members of the council may feel out-numbered and out-manoeuvred by a bloc of people. Some people may have gifts that are appropriate to the work of the team and not of the PCC (or vice versa).

Accountability is a vital issue for the team, for it must be accountable somewhere. The team must be within the official structures of the local church and not out on a limb, or worse, out of control. It should certainly give regular reports to the Annual Meeting and perhaps to the PCC as well. The PCC may refer some issues to the team for discussion with a request to report back. This helps develop a sense of a partnership between the two bodies..

The same concerns apply to relationships with the standing committee, which, after all, is charged with conducting the business of the council (albeit with qualifications) between meetings. It seems too confusing to say that the standing com-

34 David Steele, *Images of Leadership and Authority for the Church* (Lanham: University Press of America, 1986) p 146.
35 John Harvey-Jones, *Managing to Survive* (London: Heinemann, 1993) p 176.

mittee is the team (or vice versa) because it would forever be trying to remember which mode it was operating in at any given moment. Each group needs to be free to fulfil its primary function. The congregation also needs to understand the difference in function and tasks between the two.

Consideration must be given as to whether churchwardens should be part of a team. In some churches they are members by office; in some they are members in addition to their office. In at least two that I contacted they are not members and have a different role in the church. But it must be very difficult for them to perform some of their official functions if they are not members of the team.

What is worse is when one churchwarden is asked and the other is not. In some churches they are invited to attend meetings as appropriate, but this has the feel of them being 'summoned' and is not a good way of treating the church's senior lay officials. Perhaps a factor for those present and voting at the annual meeting to take into account when considering nominations of churchwardens is that they will be part of the team.

I observed a mixed experience of relationships between teams and bishops. In one case a bishop has licensed 'elders' or members of a team at their own church; in another, the bishop declined to do so. In one, the bishop declined to licence (or ordain) a team as 'permanent deacons,' responding with the suggestion that they should train as readers. He finally agreed to 'lay ministers' being commissioned by the Incumbent himself at an evening service.[36]

There will be differences in the future where a team is a diocesan requirement linked to an OLM's ministry, for which there will be an authorized service. Where teams are informally and locally constituted a certain ambivalence is bound to remain. Bishops cannot act with consistency and coherence where so many different patterns exist.

A church needs to consider whether there will be some sort of commissioning service at the setting up of a team and annual or regular renewals. Subsequently, new members of the team could simply turn up to their first meeting or the occasion might be marked by the church. Certainly some form of affirmation is good both for team members and congregation alike.

The Place of Volunteers

A leadership team will almost certainly have a mix of paid staff and volunteers (clergy and lay). Because they have chosen to be involved, volunteers provide one of the quickest indicators to whether a team is functioning well or not. Volunteers—even more than paid staff—need boundaries, fixed limits to the task, clear definitions and explanations.

As they have no legal contract, volunteers are particularly open to abuse, especially in moral pressure exerted to undertake more responsibilities. A team

36 From private correspondence.

with written job descriptions, terms of office and explicit aims and goals is likely to create higher morale than those working on unwritten or even unspoken assumptions. How to handle volunteers is worthy of further consideration and should be reviewed regularly.[37]

The Interregnum

An interregnum and the institution of a new Incumbent are stressful times for a team. They are a test of how shared the leadership has been—or a discovery that it has simply been what the outgoing Incumbent has chosen to share. A team in post by virtue of office is more likely to withstand a change of Incumbent than one too closely identified with the Incumbent who established it and chose or appointed its members.

At such a time the relationship with statutory bodies comes to the fore. It must be decided what role, if any, the team has in the process of appointing a new Incumbent. A team can feel very vulnerable, because there is no requirement for an incoming Incumbent to accept the membership or even the existence of an established team (unless it is a diocesan scheme with an OLM).

It would be revealing whether threats of disbandment brought howls of protest or resounding cheers from the congregation! That aside, the transition is a delicate process. The presence of a regular consultant would be helpful at this time.

There is a case for saying that if the church really is a pilgrim people, life moves on. What matters is not that one particular system is perpetuated but that the church has the right structure for the right time. For instance, in the 1970s and 1980s many members of teams were men in their fifties when they were appointed. Eight to ten years in that role may be quite enough. The church is at last drawing more women into leadership roles and in some places appointing younger people to leadership. The structure of a team and a team itself may have served its time.

Where I have heard of leadership teams being disbanded it is not usually followed by a retreat into clericalism. Rather, different patterns of lay ministry emerge. In one instance, a church reported that there was actually more and wider lay participation in the church since the team disappeared. The team may have left a decisive mark for good on the life of that church and have done its job.

37 Handy, *Understanding Voluntary Organizations* is worth careful study on all issues relating to handling and managing volunteers.

8

Conclusion—Is It Worth It?

So is it worth it? Yes, if you:

- have decided together as a church that a team is the right way forward for at this time;
- taken time to study the scriptural principles and grappled with the theological issues at an appropriate level;
- consulted widely with the congregation, other churches who have teams and Diocesan Ministerial Development Advisers or their equivalent;
- accepted that you cannot borrow a template of the best model but rather have understood the principles, noted good practice and heeded the warnings about pitfalls;
- consulted about the method of appointment and taken time to put it into practice;
- kept the whole congregation informed at every step of the way;
- declared publicly (best of all on paper, distributed to everyone) the aims, goals, boundaries and working practices of the team;
- built in explicit accountability of the team to the church council and/or annual meeting; and
- undertaken sustained individual and corporate, public and private prayer, that a team might truly serve the church making it more effective in mission and ministry.

Is it worth it? Yes, because a team that is working well will:

- adhere to biblical and theological principles and convictions about the nature of leadership;
- enable clergy and lay leaders to benefit from being part of a team, not working individually in lonely isolation;
- allow for far better use of gifts, skills and abilities;
- help to manage the church and offer direction more coherently and effectively than one person could alone;
- produce a better quality of recommendations;
- provide better pastoral care structures and opportunities for ministry across the church; and
- demonstrate the body of Christ at work, modelling this for the whole local church community.

It could be a monster if grossly mishandled, but it could be used for the glory of God and the building of his kingdom if time, effort and prayer are invested in its creation and management.